Richard Wagner

2 Overtures

The Flying Dutchman (Overture) /
Der fliegende Holländer (Ouvertüre)
The Mastersingers (Prelude) /
Die Meistersinger von Nürnberg (Vorspiel)

Edited by / Herausgegeben von
Egon Voss

T0081229

EULENBURG

EAS 148
ISBN 978-3-7957-6548-4
ISMN M-2002-2372-9

© 2007 Ernst Eulenburg & Co GmbH, Mainz
for Europe excluding the British Isles
Ernst Eulenburg Ltd, London
for all other countries
Edition based on RWA 104-30 and ETP 8033
CD ℗ & © 1991 Naxos Rights International Ltd

Ernst Eulenburg Ltd
48 Great Marlborough Street
London W1F 7BB

Contents / Inhalt

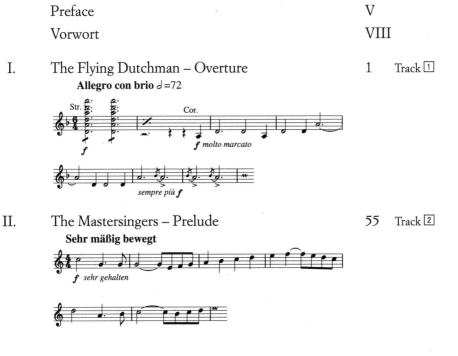

Preface

Overture: The Flying Dutchman
Composed: 5–20 November 1841 in Paris
First performance: 2 January 1843, Dresden, conducted by the composer
First publication: operatic full score, Dresden, 1844; revised overture: 1860
Orchestration: 2 flutes (piccolo), 2 oboes (cor anglais), 2 clarinets,
2 bassoons – 4 horns, 2 trumpets, 3 trombones, tuba – timpani – harp –
strings
Duration: ca. 11 minutes

Wagner's artistic interest in the legend of the Flying Dutchman was awakened during his years as Kapellmeister in Riga (1837–9). 'It was at this period that I first got to know the subject matter of *Der fliegende Holländer*', he wrote in *A Communication to my Friends*, in which he looked back on his career from the vantage point of 1851. 'The subject attracted me and left an indelible impression on me.' In his *Autobiographical Sketch* of 1842–3, Wagner additionally describes the way in which the legend suddenly acquired greater relevance for him during his voyage from Riga to London in the summer of 1839: 'This sea journey will remain forever engraved on my memory; it lasted three and a half weeks and was fraught with all manner of accidents. Three times we were caught up in the most violent storms, and on one occasion the captain was obliged to take shelter in a Norwegian harbour. Sailing between the Norwegian skerries left a curious impression on my imagination, and the legend of the Flying Dutchman, which I heard confirmed on the lips of the sailors, now took on a quite specific and individual colour in my mind.'

Wagner arrived in Paris on 17 September 1839, and between 2 and 6 May 1840 he prepared a prose draft for an opera based on the legend of the doomed seafarer. He wrote it in French with the intention of having it worked up into a libretto by one of the famous French poets of the day, hoping in turn that he would then be commissioned to set it to music for the Paris Opéra. But the commission failed to materialise, and so Wagner prepared a German libretto of his own between 18 and 28 May 1841, completing the composition draft by 22 August and putting the finishing touches to the full score of *Der fliegende Holländer* on 21 October 1841. As yet, however, the work did not include the overture, which Wagner did not begin until 5 November and which he completed by 20 November 1841 at the latest. As the last number to be written, it reflects the overture's traditional function of establishing the mood of the following opera and was based on seven of the opera's principal themes and motifs: the Dutchman's motto-like motif, with its intervals of fourths and fifths; the motif associated with the ghostly crew of the Dutchman's ship from the choral scene that opens Act Three; the motif used to depict the Dutchman's eternal wanderings; the theme heard during his opening monologue, when he expresses his longing for death; the redemption motif; the motif of fidelity in love from Senta's Ballad; and, finally, the theme of the Sailors' Chorus. As Wagner observed in a programme note that he wrote in 1853, these motifs are presented and developed in such a way that the whole plot of *Der fliegende Holländer* is recounted in purely musical terms.

The 1841 version of the overture was heard for the first time when the whole opera received its first performance in Dresden under Wagner's own direction on 2 January 1843. By the time that he conducted it at the Salle Ventadour in the Théâtre Italien in Paris seventeen years later on 25 January 1860, the overture had a different ending. This was an ending that Wagner had written earlier that same month and that he described in a letter to Karl Eckert of 21 February 1860 as 'an improvement inasmuch as it gives the whole piece a more solemn character'. This ending is also known as the 'Tristan ending', an expression suggested by Wagner himself in his letter to Mathilde Wesendonck of 10 April 1860, in which he writes that 'only now that I have written Isolde's ultimate transfiguration have I been able to find the right ending for the overture to the Flying Dutchman'. This later ending is the one that is normally heard today. Its final bars feature a further quotation of the redemption motif from Senta's Ballad, creating a sense of transfiguration as a result of the way in which the motif is formally, harmonically and instrumentally highlighted.

Prelude: The Mastersingers
Composed: 13–20 April 1862 in Biebrich, concert-ending: autumn 1862
First performance: 1 November 1862, Leipzig Gewandhaus, conducted by the composer
Original publisher: full score, B. Schott's Söhne Mainz, 1868
Orchestration: 2 flutes (piccolo), 2 oboes, 2 clarinets, 2 bassoons – 4 horns, 3 trumpets, 3 trombones, tuba – timpani, triangle, cymbals – harp – strings
Duration: ca. 10 minutes

If we may believe Wagner's reminiscences in *Mein Leben*, the initial idea for the Prelude to Act One of *Die Meistersinger von Nürnberg* came to him during a train journey from Venice to Vienna between 11 and 13 November 1861: 'It was during this journey that I was struck by the earliest musical ideas for *Die Meistersinger*; [...] I immediately conceived the main part of the overture in C major, and did so, moreover, with total clarity.' No such sketches have survived, but it is striking that immediately after returning to Vienna, Wagner set about revising the text of *Die Meistersinger*, the earliest prose draft of which dates from the summer of 1845. The libretto was completed by the end of January 1862. It may have been at this time that Wagner jotted down the earliest musical sketches, including those for the Prelude that he mentions in his autobiography: 'In the course of a beautifully sunny evening that allowed me to contemplate the magnificent view of "Golden" Mainz and the majestic Rhine flowing past it from the balcony of my apartment [in Biebrich] in a transfiguring light, the Prelude to my *Meistersinger* that had once appeared to me like some distant apparition rising up from a mood of dejection suddenly re-emerged before my soul in startling closeness and clarity. I set about writing the Prelude, just as it appears in the score today, including the main themes of the entire drama, which were already fully defined.'

The earliest tangible evidence of Wagner's work on the Prelude is an orchestral sketch which, written in the form of a short score, is dated 'Biebrich, 13 April 1862' at the beginning and '1st day of Easter [i.e., 20 April 1862]' at the end. Wagner began to work on the full score of the Prelude on 3 June 1862, taking it over into the full score of the opera, on which he worked between 1863 and 1867 and which he presented to his patron, King Ludwig II of Bavaria, at Christmas 1867.

During the time he spent in Biebrich, Wagner regularly held musical soirées, and these evidently set him thinking, prompting him to write to one of his friends in Vienna, Josef Standthartner, on 5 October 1862: 'I cannot continue to keep my works locked away as I have done in the past. And so I am now in the process of selecting passages from *Das Rheingold, Die Walküre, Der junge Siegfried, Tristan* and *Die Meistersinger* that are designed to be intelligible and effective in concert form.' From *Die Meistersinger* Wagner chose Pogner's Address, Sachs's Cobbling Song, Walther's Trial Song and the Prelude. In conversation with his second wife, Cosima, on 26 November 1879 Wagner had the following to say about this last-named piece: 'No one has yet talked, for example, about the new form of this Prelude; it is really a march with a trio, the theme of the trio appearing first in a whispered, fragmentary way before emerging as a broadly flowing melody.' During the late autumn of 1862 Wagner prepared a two-bar concert version of the ending of the Prelude comprising three chords in C major. This concert version received its first performance under Wagner's own direction at the Leipzig Gewandhaus on 1 November 1862, five and a half years before the Munich première of the opera itself. Wagner recalled the occasion in his 1869 essay, *On Conducting*: 'The first time that I performed this Prelude was at a private concert in Leipzig, [...] and it was played so well by the orchestra that the very small audience, consisting almost exclusively of friends from out of town, demanded that it should be repeated, a request to which the players, who appeared to be in entire agreement with the listeners on this point, were delighted to accede.'

Klaus Döge
Translation: Stewart Spencer

Vorwort

Ouvertüre: Der fliegende Holländer
Komponiert: 5.–20. November 1841 in Paris
Uraufführung: 2. Januar 1843, Dresden, unter der Leitung des Komponisten
Erstveröffentlichung: Opernpartitur, Dresden, 1844; revidierte Ouvertüre:
1861
Orchesterbesetzung: 2 Flöten (Piccolo), 2 Oboen (Englischhorn),
2 Klarinetten, 2 Fagotte – 4 Hörner, 2 Trompeten, 3 Posaunen, Tuba –
Pauken – Harfe – Streicher
Spieldauer: etwa 11 Minuten

Das künstlerische Interesse Richard Wagners an der Sage vom fliegenden Holländer wurde in den Rigaer Kapellmeisterjahren (1837–1839) geweckt. „In dieser Zeit lernte ich bereits den Stoff des fliegenden Holländers kennen. […] Dieser Gegenstand reizte mich und prägte sich mir unauslöschlich ein", heißt es diesbezüglich in Wagners Schaffensrückblick „Eine Mitteilung an meine Freunde" vom Jahre 1851. Und in seiner *Autobiographischen Skizze* vom Jahre 1842 beschreibt er darüber hinaus, welche Aktualität diese Sage für ihn im Sommer 1839, während seiner Schiffsreise von Riga nach Paris, angenommen hatte: „Diese Seefahrt wird mir ewig unvergesslich bleiben; sie dauerte drei und eine halbe Woche und war reich an Unfällen. Dreimal litten wir von heftigstem Sturme, und einmal sah sich der Kapitän genötigt, in einem norwegischen Hafen einzulaufen. Die Durchfahrt durch die norwegischen Schären machte einen wunderbaren Eindruck auf meine Phantasie; die Sage vom fliegenden Holländer, wie ich sie aus dem Munde der Matrosen bestätigt erhielt, gewann in mir eine bestimmte, eigentümliche Farbe."

Am 17. September 1839 traf Wagner in Paris ein und schrieb zwischen dem 2. und 6. Mai 1840 einen Opernprosaentwurf nieder, dem die Sage des fliegenden Holländers zugrunde lag. Er war in französischer Sprache verfasst, sollte von einem der damals berühmten französischen Dichter zu einem Libretto ausgearbeitet werden und Wagner den Kompositionsauftrag der Grand Opéra für dieses Libretto einbringen. Als der Auftrag aber ausblieb, verfasste Wagner zwischen dem 18. und 28. Mai 1841 ein deutschsprachiges Textbuch, schrieb bis zum 22. August den Kompositionsentwurf nieder und beendete am 21. Oktober 1841 die Partitur seines *Fliegenden Holländers*. In ihr noch nicht enthalten war die Ouvertüre, die Wagner erst am 5. November in Angriff nahm und dann spätestens am 20. November 1841 abschloss. Gemäß der traditionellen Funktion, die Stimmung der anschließenden Oper vorzubereiten, wurde die Ouvertüre als Letztes geschrieben. Sie griff die sieben wichtigsten Themen und Motive der Oper auf: das signalartige Motiv des Holländers mit seinen Quarten und

Quinten, das Motiv der geisterhaften Mannschaft vom Schiff des Holländers, das die Chorszene zu Beginn des dritten Aufzugs dominiert, das Motiv der ewigen Irrfahrt sowie das der Todessehnsucht aus dem einleitenden Monolog des Holländers, ferner das Erlösungsmotiv sowie das Motiv der Liebestreue aus Sentas Ballade und schließlich noch das Motiv des Matrosenchores. In ihrer kompositorischen Darbietung und Verarbeitung dieser Motive erzählt die Ouvertüre – wie der Komponist es 1853 in programmatischen Notizen festhielt – rein musikalisch die ganze Geschichte des fliegenden Holländers.

In der Version des Jahres 1841 erklang die Ouvertüre erstmals bei der Uraufführung der Oper am 2. Januar 1843 in Dresden unter Wagners Leitung. Als Wagner sie 17 Jahre später – am 25. Januar 1860 – in der Salle Ventadour im Gebäude der Théâtre Italien in Paris dirigierte, hatte sie einen anderen Schluss. Diesen hatte Wagner im Januar 1860 neu komponiert und nannte ihn, wie es im Brief an Karl Eckert vom 21. Februar 1860 zu lesen ist, einen „besseren Schluss zur Ouvertüre", da er „dem Ganzen einen weihevolleren Charakter giebt." Dieser Schluss ist auch bekannt als „Tristan-Schluss", ein Ausdruck, den Wagner selbst in einem Brief an Mathilde Wesendonck vom 10. April 1860 verwendete. Dort heißt es: „Jetzt, wo ich Isoldes letzte Verklärung geschrieben, konnte ich […] erst den rechten Schluß zur Fliegenden-Holländer-Ouvertüre […] finden." Dieser kommt heute für gewöhnlich zur Aufführung. Formal, harmonisch und instrumentatorisch exponiert, zitiert Wagner in dessen letzten, so verklärend wirkenden Takten noch einmal das Motiv der Erlösung aus Sentas Ballade.

Vorspiel: Die Meistersinger von Nürnberg
Komponiert: 13.–20. April in Biebrich, Konzertschluss: Herbst 1862
Uraufführung: 1. November 1862, Leipziger Gewandhaus, unter der
Leitung des Komponisten
Originalverlag: Partitur, B. Schott's Söhne Mainz, 1868
Orchesterbesetzung: 2 Flöten (Piccolo), 2 Oboen, 2 Klarinetten,
2 Fagotte – 4 Hörner, 3 Trompeten, 3 Posaunen, Tuba – Pauken, Triangel,
Becken – Harfe – Streicher
Spieldauer: etwa 10 Minuten

Folgt man Wagners Erinnerungen in seiner Autobiographie *Mein Leben*, so entstanden die ersten Ideen zum *Meistersinger*-Vorspiel auf der Zugreise von Venedig nach Wien zwischen dem 11. und 13. November 1861: „Während der Fahrt gingen mir die ‚Meistersinger' […] zuerst musikalisch auf; ich konzipierte sofort mit größter Deutlichkeit den Hauptteil der Ouvertüre in C-Dur." Entsprechende Noten-Niederschriften dazu sind nicht erhalten, doch ist auffällig, dass Wagner unmittelbar nach seiner Ankunft in Wien begann, den Text der *Meistersinger*, zu denen er einst im Sommer 1845 einen ersten Prosaentwurf verfasst hatte, weiter auszuarbeiten und das Werk bis Ende Januar 1862 in Gedichtform zu bringen. Möglicherweise notierte Wagner bereits in dieser Phase erste musikalische Skizzen, darunter vielleicht auch jene zum Vorspiel, von der er in *Mein Leben* spricht: „Bei einem schönen Sonnenuntergange, welcher mich von dem Balkon meiner Wohnung [in Biebrich] aus den prachtvollen Anblick des ‚Goldenen' Mainz mit dem vor ihm dahinströmenden majestätischen Rhein in verklärender Beleuchtung betrachten ließ, trat auch plötzlich das Vorspiel zu meinen ‚Meistersingern', wie ich es einst aus trüber Stimmung als fernes Luftbild vor mir erscheinen gesehen hatte, nahe und deutlich wieder vor die Seele. Ich ging daran, das Vorspiel aufzuzeichnen, und zwar ganz so, wie es heute in der Partitur steht, demnach die Hauptmotive des ganzen Dramas mit größter Bestimmtheit in sich fassend."

Erstmals in einer musikalischen Quelle greifbar wird das Vorspiel in der particellmäßig geschriebenen Orchesterskizze. Als Anfangsdatum erscheint dort: „Biebrich. 13. April 1862.", und das Datum der Beendigung des Vorspiels lautet ebenda: „1. Osterfeiertag" [= 20. April 1862]. Eine erste Partiturniederschrift erfolgte am 3. Juni 1862; danach wurde es in die zwischen 1863 und 1867 angefertigte Meistersinger-Partitur übernommen, die Wagner Weihnachten 1867 seinem Mäzen König Ludwig II. von Bayern schenkte.

Angeregt von den Musikabenden in seinem Biebricher Domizil, fasste Wagner einen Entschluss, den er am 5. Oktober 1862 sogleich seinem Wiener Freund Josef Standthartner brieflich mitteilte: „Ich kann meine neuen Werke nicht fernerhin so secretiren lassen, wie dies bisher geschehen. Demnach bin ich jetzt darüber her, aus dem ‚Rheingold', der ‚Walküre' dem ‚jungen Siegfried' ‚Tristan' und den ‚Meistersingern' solche Fragmente auszuwählen, welche in einer großen Concertaufführung sich verständlich und wirksam ausnehmen sollen." Aus den *Meistersingern von Nürnberg* wählte er dabei neben Pogners Ansprache, dem Schusterlied und Walthers Probelied auch das Vorspiel aus, das er am 26. November 1879 Cosima gegenüber in den Tagebüchern mit den Worten charakterisierte: „Noch niemand hat z. B. über die neue Form dieses Vorspieles gesprochen, es ist eigentlich ein Marsch mit einem Trio, wo das Thema des Trio zuerst flüsternd unterbrochen auftritt, bis es dann in seiner Breite erscheint." Für die von der Oper losgelöste Einzelaufführung schrieb er im Herbst 1862 eigens jenen zweitaktigen Konzertschluss (drei Akkorde in C-Dur), mit dem das *Meistersinger*-Vorspiel am 1. November 1862 – fünfeinhalb Jahre vor der Münchner Premiere der Oper selbst – im Konzert des Leipziger Gewandhauses unter der Leitung des Komponisten seine Uraufführung erlebte. In seinem Aufsatz *Über das Dirigieren* aus dem Jahre 1869 erinnerte Wagner sich daran: „Dieses Vorspiel führte ich zum ersten mal in einem in Leipzig gegebenen Privatkonzerte auf, und es wurde […] vom Orchester so vorzüglich gespielt, daß das sehr kleine, fast nur aus auswärtigen Freunden meiner Musik bestehende, Auditorium lebhaft eine sofortige Wiederholung verlangte, welche von den Musikern, da sie hierin ganz mit den Zuhörern übereinzustimmen schienen, mit freudiger Bereitwilligkeit ausgeführt wurde."

Klaus Döge

Der fliegende Holländer – Ouvertüre
The Flying Dutchman – Overture

Richard Wagner
(1813–1883)

© 2007 Ernst Eulenburg Ltd, London
and Ernst Eulenburg & Co GmbH, Mainz

2

4

6

8

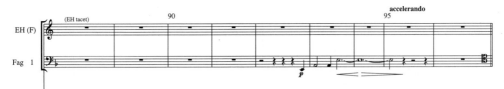

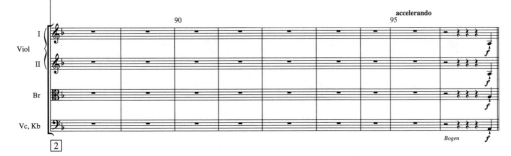

12

14

15

16

18

20

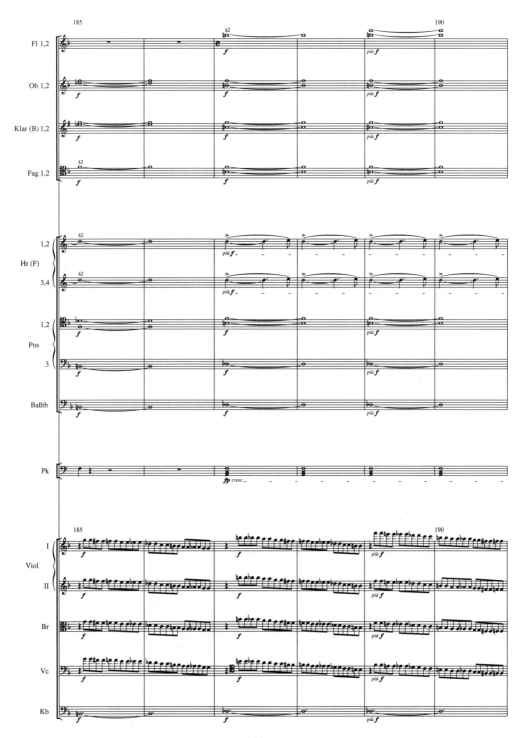

22

24

28

30

32

34

36

EAS 148

38

41

EAS 148

42

44

48

EAS 148

50

51

EAS 148

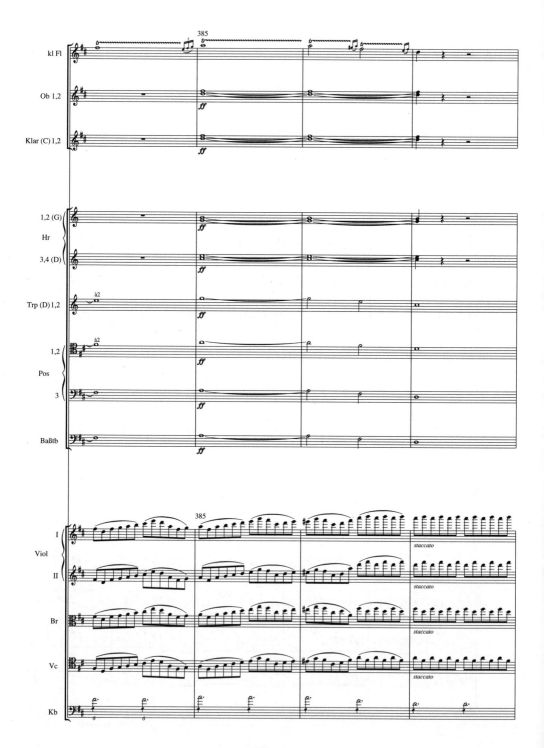

54

EAS 148

Die Meistersinger von Nürnberg – Vorspiel
The Mastersingers – Prelude

Richard Wagner
(1813–1883)

EAS 148

© 2007 Ernst Eulenburg Ltd, London and Ernst Eulenburg & Co GmbH, Mainz

56

57

60

62

EAS 148

64

66

69

EAS 148

70

72

74

80

EAS 148

82

84

EAS 148

90

EAS 148

92

93

95

EAS 148

Printed in China